W9-CPC-950

DISCARD

DATE DUE

PRINTED IN U S A

THE EMANCIPATION PROCLAMATION, LINCOLN, AND SLAVERY THROUGH PRIMARY SOURCES

Carin T. Ford

Enslow Publishers, Inc.
40 Industrial Road
Box 398
Berkeley Heights, NJ 07922
USA

http://www.enslow.com

Original edition published as *Lincoln, Slavery, and the Emancipation Proclamation* in 2004.

Library of Congress Cataloging-in-Publication Data
Ford, Carin T.
  The Emancipation Proclamation, Lincoln, and slavery through primary sources / Carin T. Ford.
      p. cm. — (The Civil War through primary sources)
  "Original edition published as Lincoln, Slavery, and the Emancipation Proclamation in 2004."
  Includes bibliographical references and index.
  Summary: "Examines the roots of slavery in America and how the issue divided the nation, as well as the start of the Civil War, President Lincoln's views on slavery, and his first step toward ending it forever: the Emancipation Proclamation"—Provided by publisher.
  ISBN 978-0-7660-4129-5
  1. Lincoln, Abraham, 1809-1865—Views on slavery—Juvenile literature. 2. Slavery—United States—History—Juvenile literature. 3. Slaves—Emancipation—United States—Juvenile literature. 4. United States. President (1861–1865 : Lincoln). Emancipation Proclamation—Juvenile literature. 5. United States—Politics and government—1861–1865—Juvenile literature. I. Ford, Carin T. Lincoln, slavery, and the Emancipation Proclamation. II. Title.
  E457.2.F68 2014
  973.7'14—dc23

                    2012036351

Future editions:
Paperback ISBN: 978-1-4644-0187-9
EPUB ISBN: 978-1-4645-1100-4
Single-User PDF ISBN: 978-1-4646-1100-1
Multi-User PDF ISBN: 978-0-7660-5729-6

Printed in China

012013 Leo Paper Group, Heshan City, Guangdong, China

10 9 8 7 6 5 4 3 2 1

To Our Readers: We have done our best to make sure all Internet Addresses in this book were active and appropriate when we went to press. However, the author and the publisher have no control over and assume no liability for the material available on those Internet sites or on other Web sites they may link to. Any comments or suggestions can be sent by email to comments@enslow.com or to the address on the back cover.

Illustration Credits: Enslow Publishers, Inc., pp. 14, 22; Library of Congress Prints and Photographs, pp. 1, 2, 3, 5, 6, 7, 8, 10, 11, 16, 18, 19, 20, 21, 24, 27, 28, 30, 32, 33, 34, 35, 39, 40; Library of Congress Rare Books and Manuscripts Division, p. 13; National Archives and Records Administration, pp. 4, 37; Shutterstock.com, p. 26.

Cover Illustration: Library of Congress Prints and Photographs (Foreground, Abraham Lincoln portrait, November 1863) and National Archives and Records Administration (Background, page one of the Emancipation Proclamation).

CONTENTS

LOOK FOR THIS SYMBOL  TO FIND THE PRIMARY SOURCES THROUGHOUT THIS BOOK.

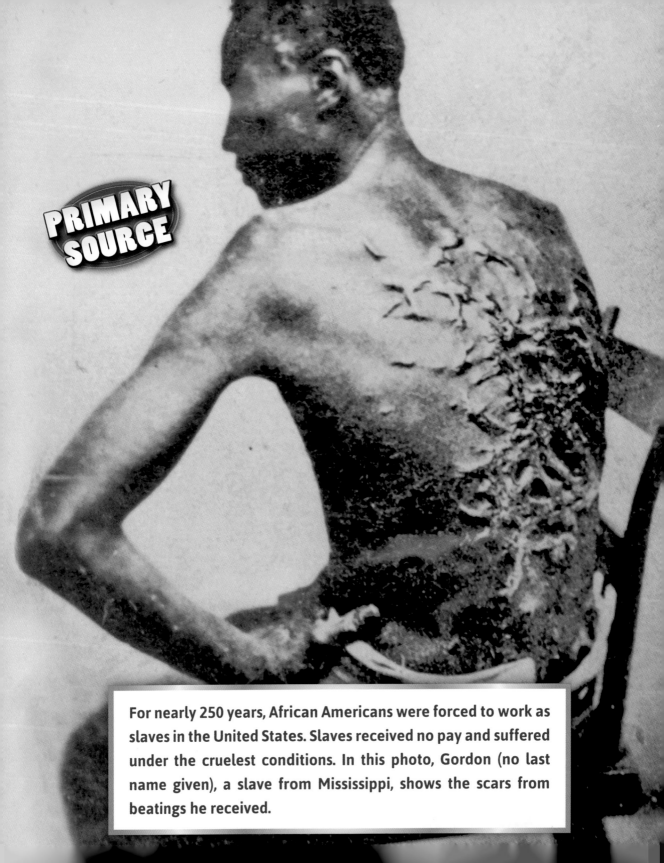

For nearly 250 years, African Americans were forced to work as slaves in the United States. Slaves received no pay and suffered under the cruelest conditions. In this photo, Gordon (no last name given), a slave from Mississippi, shows the scars from beatings he received.

CHAPTER 1

SLAVERY TAKES ROOT

"If slavery is not wrong, nothing is wrong."[1] When Abraham Lincoln wrote these words, Americans were bitterly divided over slavery. For nearly 250 years, black slaves had worked hard on farms and plantations, mainly in the South. Slaves were bought and sold like property. Their owners did not pay them for their work. Many slaves were beaten with whips and given little food or clothing.

The businesses, factories, and small farms of the North did not need slave labor, and many Northerners had come to believe that slavery was wrong. They wanted to put an end to it. The large plantations of the South depended on the work of slaves, and

Abraham Lincoln first witnessed the brutality of slavery growing up near the Cumberland Trail. This is an 1868 illustration of young Abraham reading in his log cabin.

Slaves wearing handcuffs and shackles pass through Washington, D.C., around 1815. The journey of blacks from Africa to the slave market in North America was extremely harsh. Many died along the way. Once slaves arrived in America, their treatment did not improve.

most Southerners wanted to keep slavery. As president, Lincoln did more than anyone before him to free the 4 million black slaves from their chains.

Lincoln was born February 12, 1809, near Hodgenville, Kentucky. He came from a poor family of pioneers. They moved often, throughout the West.

In this 1862 photo, African-American slaves work in a pile of cotton, preparing it for the cotton gin at Smith's plantation in Port Royal Island, South Carolina. The thriving cotton industry demanded more and more slave labor.

Lincoln grew up near the Cumberland Trail, which ran from Louisville, Kentucky, to Nashville, Tennessee. Pioneers, preachers, and peddlers made their way along the trail. There were also slaves, tied together by the hands and feet, traveling on the trail. This is probably where young Abraham Lincoln saw slaves for the first time.[2]

The first African slaves were brought to America in 1619. Traders from Europe made a lot of money selling slaves. Men, women, and children were kidnapped in Africa, chained, and shipped across the Atlantic Ocean to America. Millions died on the long journey across the sea. Through the years, the number of slaves in America grew slowly.

That suddenly changed when Eli Whitney invented the cotton gin in 1793. The machine removed the seeds from cotton. With a machine doing the work instead of a person, farmers could now clean fifty times more cotton each day.

Southern farmers could make a great deal of money selling this crop. Many of them quickly switched to growing cotton.

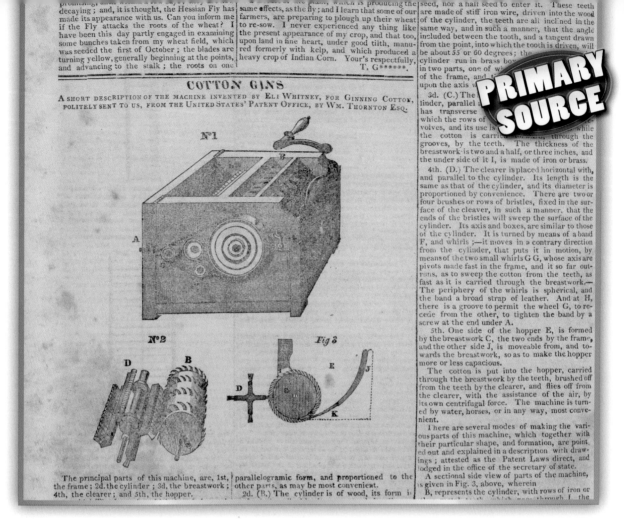

The cotton gin, shown in this 1823 illustration from the publication *American Farmer*, forever changed slavery in the South.

More slaves than ever were needed to work in the fields, planting and picking cotton.

By 1830, the number of slaves had climbed to more than 2 million, and slavery had become a major part of life in the United States.[3]

CHAPTER 2

★

THE BATTLE OVER SLAVERY

In 1828, Abraham Lincoln traveled on a flatboat down the Mississippi River to New Orleans, Louisiana. The boat was carrying farm products to market. As legend tells the story, Lincoln, age nineteen, now got a closer look at slavery. Slaves in chains were being whipped. Black men, women, and children were being sold like cattle at auctions. Lincoln began to feel a deep hatred of slavery.[1]

Lincoln was not the only one in the country who felt strongly about slavery. Mostly in the North, there were many people who wanted to abolish—or put an end to—slavery. They were called abolitionists.

William Lloyd Garrison was an abolitionist who published an antislavery newspaper. He called it *The Liberator*. The word *liberate* means "to set free."

"I will not retreat a single inch—*and I will be heard*," wrote Garrison in the newspaper's first issue.[2] Garrison's voice was heard for the next thirty-five years. He also spread his views by helping form the American Anti-Slavery Society in 1833. Members of the society gave speeches and wrote newspaper and magazine articles calling for an end to slavery.

Many people in the South were angry about these antislavery groups. Southerners asked the Northern lawmakers to put a stop to them. People in the South did not want slavery to end. The cotton industry needed slaves.

Lincoln was a member of the Illinois House of Representatives at this time. In 1837, Illinois's lawmakers voted to stop antislavery activity. Only six lawmakers voted in favor of the abolitionists. Lincoln was one of them. He wrote that slavery was based on "injustice and bad policy."[3] Still, he said that Congress did not have the power to end slavery in states where it already existed.

THE LIBERATOR.

VOL. I.] WILLIAM LLOYD GARRISON AND ISAAC KNAPP, PUBLISHERS. **[NO. 21.**

BOSTON, MASSACHUSETTS.] OUR COUNTRY IS THE WORLD—OUR COUNTRYMEN ARE MANKIND. [SATURDAY, MAY 21, 1831.

William Lloyd Garrison, an abolitionist, founded the anti-slavery newspaper, *The Liberator*, in 1831. His outspoken views against slavery were not received well in the South.

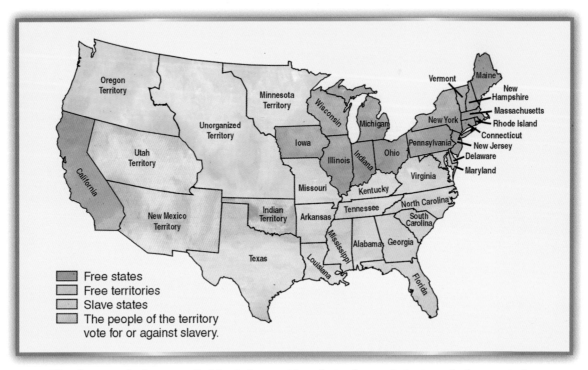

Free states
Free territories
Slave states
The people of the territory
vote for or against slavery.

The issue of slavery divided the nation into free states and slave states. Pro-slavery supporters wanted new states entering the Union to allow slavery, while abolitionists wanted those states to prohibit slavery. The Missouri Compromise and the Compromise of 1850 left neither side happy.

It was the first time Lincoln spoke out in public against slavery. But it was far from his last.

After his term in the Illinois Congress ended, Lincoln returned to his law practice. In 1841, Lincoln was the lawyer for a woman who had been sold into slavery in Illinois. He won her freedom by arguing that Illinois was not a slave state, so a person could not be bought or sold there.

Lincoln was elected for a two-year term in the United States Congress. As a congressman, from 1847 to 1849, he was rather quiet on the issue of slavery. At one point, he said that he would suggest a law to free the slaves in Washington, D.C., but he did not follow through on this.

In 1820, the Missouri Compromise allowed Maine to enter the Union as a free state and said Missouri would be a slave state. That kept an equal number of slave states and free states.

Congress was working hard to satisfy both the abolitionists of the North and the slave owners of the South. The Compromise of 1850 brought in California as a free state and banned the slave trade in the District of Columbia (although slavery was still allowed there). For the South, it made stricter punishments for anyone helping a runaway slave. Neither the North nor the South thought the Compromise of 1850 was fair.

When Lincoln ran for a seat in the U.S. Senate in 1858, slavery was an important issue to the voters. Even more new territories and states were being settled in the West. Should slavery be allowed in these areas?

The portrait of Abraham Lincoln (left) was taken on October 1, 1858, two weeks before the final Lincoln-Douglas debate. The photo of Stephen A. Douglas (top) was taken sometime between 1844 and 1860. Lincoln's unsuccessful senate campaign was an important point in his political career.

Lincoln believed the answer was no. He said it could stay in the states where it already existed, but he thought that over time, slavery would come to an end by itself.

The man Lincoln was running against for the Senate was Stephen A. Douglas. Lincoln and Douglas argued often about slavery. In Douglas's opinion, the people in each area should decide for themselves whether or not to allow slavery.

Lincoln did not agree. He called slavery "the disease of the entire nation."[4] He feared that Douglas's plan would spread slavery throughout the American West.

Lincoln always worried that slavery might split the country in two. In a famous speech, he used a quote from the Bible: "A house divided against itself cannot stand." He went on to say that the country "will become all one thing, or all the other."[5] He was saying that one day, the whole country would either abolish slavery or allow it.

Lincoln lost the election to Douglas, yet his speeches against slavery were remembered.

This is a banner from Abraham Lincoln's first campaign for president. When Lincoln was elected in November 1860, the South, fearful of Lincoln's anti-slavery beliefs, decided to take action.

In 1860, Lincoln ran for president. He did not win many votes in the Southern slave states. The votes for Lincoln came from the eighteen free states. Lincoln's problems began immediately after he won the election. Southerners knew that he was against the spread of slavery. They were afraid that as president he would try to get rid of slavery in the whole country. So they decided to take action.

CHAPTER 3

---⭐---

A NATION TORN APART

South Carolina was the first state to break away—or secede—from the United States in December 1860. Six more southern states (Mississippi, Florida, Alabama, Georgia, Louisiana, and Texas) soon followed. They formed their own country—the Confederate States of America—with its own government.

Lincoln was sworn in as the sixteenth president of the United States on March 4, 1861. President Lincoln did not want the nation torn apart. "Can this country be saved?" he had asked before taking office. "If it can, I will consider myself one of the happiest men in the world if I can help to save it."[1]

Inauguration of Abraham Lincoln - March 4, 1861.

A view of President Abraham Lincoln's inauguration in front of the U.S. Capitol on March 4, 1861. By the time Lincoln was sworn in as president, several Southern states had already seceded from the Union.

Fighting broke out when Confederate soldiers in South Carolina attacked Fort Sumter on April 12, 1861. The fort belonged to the U.S. government. With few men or supplies, it was forced to surrender. After this, four more states (Virginia, Arkansas, North Carolina, and Tennessee) seceded from the United States, bringing the total of Confederate States to eleven.

This photo taken on April 15, 1861, shows the interior of Fort Sumter after the Confederate capture of it. The Confederate flag can be seen at the top of the image. This was the first battle of the Civil War.

Who's Who in The Civil War

★ The North was also known as the Union, or the United States. The people there were often called Yankees.

★ The South was called the Confederate States, or the Confederacy. During the war, Southerners were also called Rebels or Johnny Reb.

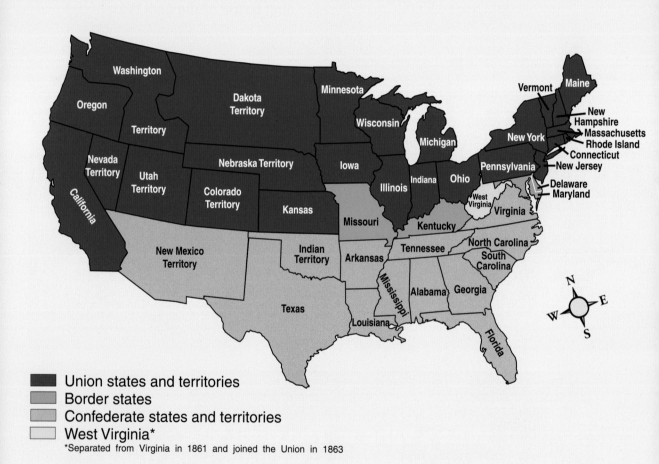

Union states and territories
Border states
Confederate states and territories
West Virginia*
*Separated from Virginia in 1861 and joined the Union in 1863

This map shows the division between the Union and the Confederacy during the Civil War. Several border states sided with the North, despite being slave states. President Lincoln worried that if he freed the slaves, these states might leave and join the Confederacy.

Although he had hoped to avoid war, Lincoln now called for 75,000 men to join the Union army. The Civil War had begun.

From the start, Lincoln said the war was being fought to save the country, not to destroy slavery. "If I could save the Union without freeing *any* slave I would do it, and if I could save it by freeing all the slaves I would do it; . . . What I do about slavery, and the colored race," he wrote, "I do because it helps to save the Union."[2]

Lincoln believed that most Union soldiers were fighting to save their country. He did not think they would be willing to risk their lives to free the slaves.[3]

Still, the growing number of abolitionists in the North wanted Lincoln to end slavery right away. Lincoln believed slavery was wrong—but he also believed in upholding the laws of the United States. He was not sure the U.S. Constitution gave him the power to abolish slavery. It had always been a matter that each state decided for itself.

Lincoln was also worried about Kentucky, Missouri, Maryland, and Delaware. These states were on the border of the North and

A year into the Civil War, President Lincoln said, "Things had gone on from bad to worse." This was the last "beardless" portrait taken of Lincoln on August 13, 1860, shortly before he was elected president.

the South. They were loyal to the Union—but they allowed slavery. Would they join the Confederacy if Lincoln got rid of slavery?

Kentucky led the way to the West, as well as to the heart of the Confederacy. "I think to lose Kentucky is nearly the same as to lose the whole game," Lincoln said.[4]

After a year of fighting, the North had lost a lot of men and was not winning many battles. "Things had gone on from bad to worse," Lincoln said.[5] He decided the time had come to free the slaves. Lincoln said it was a "military necessity" if he hoped to put the country back together.[6]

Lincoln believed that freeing—or emancipating—the slaves would hurt the Confederacy. For one thing, the South's cotton fields would lose most of its workers if there were no slaves. For another, these former slaves would be able to join the Union army. This would help the North.

One morning in June 1862, Lincoln visited the telegraph office of the War Department. The telegraph was a machine for sending messages. It was used in the days before the telephone was invented. Lincoln wanted to see the reports on how the Union

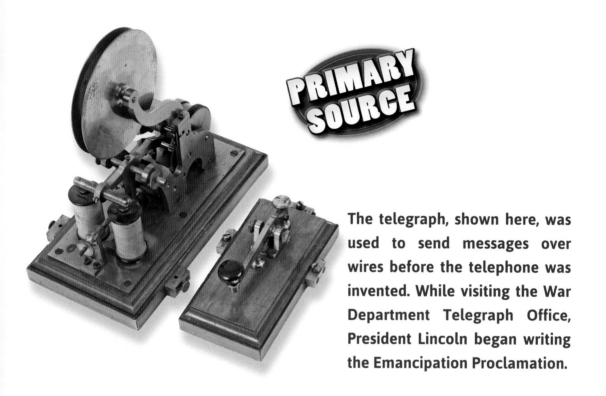

PRIMARY SOURCE

The telegraph, shown here, was used to send messages over wires before the telephone was invented. While visiting the War Department Telegraph Office, President Lincoln began writing the Emancipation Proclamation.

army was doing. It was a quiet place, and Lincoln knew he could work there without being disturbed. Thomas T. Eckert was the head of the office. He said Lincoln came in one day and asked for a piece of paper "to write something special."[7]

Lincoln was about to begin writing the Emancipation Proclamation. *Emancipation* means freedom. A *proclamation* is a public announcement.

CHAPTER 4

TAKING ACTION

Eckert remembered the day Lincoln began writing this paper: "He would look out the window a while and then put his pen to paper, but he did not write much at once," Eckert said. "He would study between times and when he had made up his mind he would put down a line or two, and then sit quiet for a few minutes."[1]

That day, when Lincoln was finished, he handed Eckert the paper and asked him to hold on to it. Lincoln had not filled even one sheet.

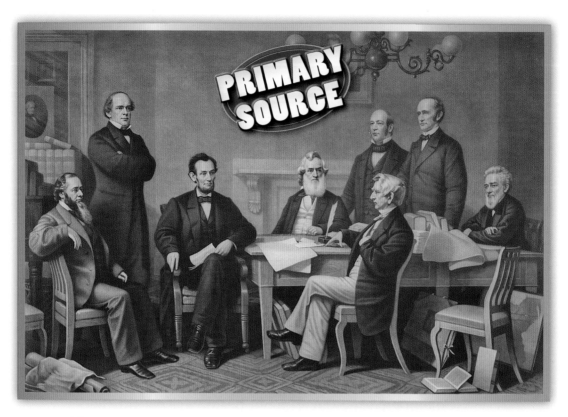

This engraving was created from a painting by F. B. Carpenter called "The First Reading of the Emancipation Proclamation Before the Cabinet."

For the next few weeks, Lincoln came to the telegraph office each day. Eckert would take out the papers, which he kept in a locked desk, and hand them to the president.

Lincoln did not tell Eckert what he was working on until he had finished. Then Lincoln explained that he was freeing the slaves in the South. He said this would end the war more quickly.

Lincoln's Emancipation Proclamation stated that all the slaves in the rebelling states were being set free.[2] The Emancipation Proclamation also said that African Americans would be allowed to join the U.S. army and navy.

In July 1862, Lincoln asked other lawmakers for advice about the Emancipation Proclamation. Some liked it. Others worried that there were many Northerners who might be upset. Even though most people in the North believed slavery was wrong, many of them did not think black people were equal to whites. They did not think blacks should have the same rights as white people, and they did not want the 4 million African-American slaves to be set free.

Lincoln said he was "afraid that half the officers [in the Union army] would fling down their arms" and refuse to fight when they heard about his plan to free the slaves.[3]

Secretary of State William H. Seward was pleased with the proclamation. But he told Lincoln not to issue it right away. The people in the North were not happy about how the war was going. The Union army had not won a key battle in a long while.

PRIMARY SOURCE

Secretary of State William H. Seward gave President Lincoln advice about when to issue the Emancipation Proclamation.

Seward thought it might look as if Lincoln had written the Emancipation Proclamation just so African Americans could help fight in the Union army.

Seward told Lincoln to wait until the North had won a big victory.[4] Lincoln agreed, and he waited. On September 17, 1862, the battle of Antietam took place near Sharpsburg, Maryland. It was the single bloodiest day of fighting in American history. More than 23,000 men were killed or wounded. The battle was terrible, but it was a victory for the North.

The President's Wartime Power

Could President Lincoln end slavery without disobeying the U.S. Constitution? As the Civil War went on, Lincoln decided the answer was yes. As president, he was commander-in-chief of the army and navy—and the Constitution gave him wartime powers against his enemies. He could free the slaves to hurt the Confederacy and help the United States win the war. In his proclamation, he called freeing the slaves "an act of justice."[5] He was glad to be doing a good deed, too.

As William Seward had suggested, President Lincoln waited until after an important Union victory before issuing the Emancipation Proclamation. Despite heavy Union losses at Antietam, Lincoln felt he had the victory he needed. This photo shows the president (center) at Union camp in Antietam on October 3, 1862.

In this illustration, Union and Confederate soldiers clash at the Battle of Antietam, the single bloodiest day of fighting in American history.

Five days later, on September 22, 1862, Lincoln published a draft of his proclamation—called the Preliminary Emancipation Proclamation.

Lincoln gave a warning to the Confederate States: If they did not come back into the Union by January 1, 1863, the Emancipation Proclamation would take effect, freeing all slaves in the rebelling Southern states.

CHAPTER 5

LET FREEDOM RING

"**I** never, in my life, felt more certain that I was doing right than I do in signing this paper," Lincoln said of the Emancipation Proclamation.[1]

In truth, issuing the Emancipation Proclamation did not free a single slave. Lincoln said the slaves in the rebelling states were now free. But the Confederates did not obey Lincoln. Jefferson Davis was their president. Lincoln had no power in the Confederacy.

The proclamation would succeed only if the North won the war and the country was put back together. Then Lincoln would have the power to end slavery throughout the United States.

Ent'd according to Act of Congress, A. D. 1863, by W. T. Carlton, in the Clerk's Office of the District Court of the District of Mass.

African-American men, women, and children gather at a watch meeting on December 31, 1862, waiting for the hour to strike midnight, when the Emancipation Proclamation would take effect.

Waiting for the Proclamation

On December 31, 1862, a large crowd gathered in Boston. They were waiting for midnight, when the Emancipation Proclamation would officially take effect. Among them were abolitionists William Lloyd Garrison, Harriet Beecher Stowe, and Frederick Douglass, who was weeping with joy.[2] All over, other people waited, too, as in the scene above.

Lincoln also had a plan to deal with slaves in the Border States that remained loyal to the Union. He said that the government would pay slave owners if they gave up their slaves.

The Emancipation Proclamation was important because it showed the world that the Civil War was now being fought to end slavery. It also gave hope to millions of black Americans.

Many people cheered when they heard about it. Horace Greeley, editor of the *New York Tribune*, wrote that it was "the beginning of the new life of the nation."[3] Black Americans were especially happy. "We shout with joy," said Frederick Douglass, an ex-slave who became a leading spokesman for African Americans.[4]

Crowds of people—both black and white—stood outside the White House singing, clapping, and calling out for the president. They believed the Emancipation Proclamation was a symbol of freedom.

Of course, not everyone was pleased. In the Confederacy, President Jefferson Davis called it one of the most horrible acts in history.[5] Many Northerners were unhappy that the war was now being fought over slavery.

By the President of the United States of America:

A Proclamation.

Whereas, on the twenty-second day of September, in the year of our Lord one thousand eight hundred and sixty-two, a proclamation was issued by the President of the United States, containing, among other things, the following, to wit:

"That on the first day of January, in the year of our Lord one thousand eight hundred and sixty-three, all persons held as slaves within any State or designated part of a State, the people whereof shall then be in rebellion against the United States, shall be then, thenceforward, and forever free; and the Executive Government of the United States, including the military and naval authority thereof, will recognize and maintain the freedom of such persons, and will do no act or acts to repress such persons, or any of them, in any efforts they may make for their actual freedom.

"That the Executive will, on the first day

This is page one of the Emancipation Proclamation, the document granting freedom to slaves in the rebelling Southern states.

As a result of the Emancipation Proclamation, thousands of African Americans fled from the South. Both slaves and free blacks headed North to join the Union army. By war's end, nearly 200,000 African Americans would fight for the Union. Twenty-four would receive the Congressional Medal of Honor.

When Lincoln was elected for another term as president in November 1864, he looked old and tired. There were many new wrinkles on his face. The war had been very hard on him.

Black Soldiers

★ Many whites did not like the idea of fighting to free black Americans. "You say you will not fight to free Negroes," said Lincoln. "Some of them seem willing to fight for you."[6]

★ A Kentucky soldier said he "volunteered to fight to restore the Old Constitution and not to free the Negroes and we are not going to do it."[7]

★ Some white soldiers were glad blacks were joining the army. "If they can kill rebels I say arm them and set them to shooting," said one soldier from Illinois.[8]

In this photo taken between 1863 and 1865, an unidentified African-American Union soldier stands in full uniform with a bayoneted musket.

He wanted nothing more than peace. Lincoln hoped to "bind up the nation's wounds," he said.[9]

When Confederate general Robert E. Lee surrendered to Union general Ulysses S. Grant on April 9, 1865, the end of the Civil War was finally in sight. The war had lasted four bloody years. More than 600,000 lives had been lost.

At last, 4 million African Americans were now free. That same year, in December, the Thirteenth Amendment to the

This "$100,000 Reward" poster was issued for the capture of the murderer and conspirators in President Lincoln's assassination. John Wilkes Booth (top center of poster) was killed during an attempt to capture him twelve days after the murder.

U.S. Constitution was passed. Slavery was now against the law in every state of the country.

Five nights after General Lee surrendered, Lincoln was shot. He had been watching a play at Ford's Theater in Washington, D.C. The killer was John Wilkes Booth, an actor who had wanted the South to win the war. He was violently angry with President Lincoln for freeing the slaves. Booth was found and killed twelve days later by federal troops.

Lincoln lived through the night, but he died the next morning. It was April 15, 1865, and he was fifty-six years old. Thousands of people gathered to say good-bye as a train carried Lincoln's body back to Springfield, Illinois.

African Americans were now facing a long struggle to be treated as equal human beings. Issuing the Emancipation Proclamation was only the beginning—but it was an important beginning.

President Lincoln was extremely proud of the Emancipation Proclamation. He once said, "If my name ever goes into history, it will be for this act."[10]

TIMELINE

1600s

1619: African slaves are sold in Jamestown, Virginia.

1662: Virginia law states that slaves from Africa will remain slaves for life.

1700s

1774: Northern states begin to abolish slavery.

1793: The cotton gin is invented, giving new life to the slave industry in the South.

1800s

1808: Importing slaves from other countries is outlawed.

1809: Abraham Lincoln is born in near Hodgenville, Kentucky.

1818: Ten states allow slavery and ten do not.

1820: Missouri Compromise says Maine will be a free state, Missouri a slave state.

1831: William Lloyd Garrison begins publishing *The Liberator*.

1834: Lincoln is elected to the Illinois House of Representatives.

1841: Lincoln returns to his private law practice.

1846: Lincoln is elected to the U.S. House of Representatives.

1850: New law sets stricter punishments for people helping runaway slaves.

1858: Lincoln runs for the U.S. Senate against Stephen Douglas, and the two men debate over the issue of slavery. Lincoln loses the election.

1860: Lincoln becomes president of the United States; South Carolina secedes from the United States.

1861: Six more Southern states secede, and the Confederate States of America is formed, with Jefferson Davis as president; the Civil War begins, and four more Southern states join the Confederacy.

1862: Lincoln begins working on the Emancipation Proclamation. He publishes the Preliminary Emancipation Proclamation on September 22.

1863: Lincoln issues the Emancipation Proclamation on January 1, freeing slaves in the rebelling states.

1864: Lincoln is reelected to a second term as president.

1865: Confederate general Lee surrenders to Union general Grant.

• President Lincoln is assassinated.

• Andrew Johnson becomes president.

• The rest of the Confederate armies surrender, and the Civil War is over.

• The Thirteenth Amendment to the Constitution is passed, abolishing slavery in the United States.

CHAPTER NOTES

CHAPTER 1. SLAVERY TAKES ROOT

1. Roy P. Basler, ed., *Lincoln: Speeches and Writings 1859–1865* (New Brunswick, N.J.: Rutgers University Press, 1974, p. 585.

2. *The American Presidency: Abraham Lincoln Biography*, n.d., <http://gi.grolier.com/presidents/ea/bios/16plinc.html> (October 22, 2003).

3. *Abstract of the Returns of the Fifth Census* (Washington, D.C.: Duff Gree, 1832), p. 47.

CHAPTER 2. THE BATTLE OVER SLAVERY

1. William H. Herndon and Jesse W. Weik, *Herndon's Life of Lincoln* (New York: Da Capo Press, 1983), p. 64.

2. "The Liberator, 'To the Public,' 1831," *Africans in America*, n.d., <http://www.pbs.org/wgbh/aia/part4/4h2928.html> (October 22, 2003).

3. Herndon and Weik, p. 144.

4. William K. Klingaman, *Abraham Lincoln and the Road to Emancipation, 1861–1865* (New York: Viking Penguin, 2001), p. 8.

5. "A House Divided Against Itself Cannot Stand," *National Center for Public Policy Research*, n.d., <http://www.nationalcenter.org/HouseDivided.html> (October 22, 2003).

CHAPTER 3. A NATION TORN APART

1. Ralph Geoffrey Newman, ed., *Abraham Lincoln: His Story in His Own Words* (Garden City, N.Y.: Doubleday & Company, Inc., 1975), p. 61.

2. National Park Service, *National UGRR Network to Freedom Program*, n.d., <http://www.cr.nps.gov/ugrr/learn_a6.htm> (October 22, 2003).

3. William K. Klingaman, *Abraham Lincoln and the Road to Emancipation, 1861–1865* (New York: Viking Penguin, 2001), p. 140.

4. Ibid., p. 50.

5. Ibid., p. 139.

6. Stephen B. Oates, *With Malice Toward None: The Life of Abraham Lincoln* (New York: Harper & Row, 1977), p. 309.

7. Klingaman, p. 139.

CHAPTER 4. TAKING ACTION

1. John Hope Franklin, *The Emancipation Proclamation* (Garden City, N.Y.: Doubleday & Company, Inc., 1963), p. 35.

2. "The Emancipation Proclamation," *National Park Service*, n.d., <http://www .nps.gov/ncro/anti/emancipation.html> (October 22, 2003).

3. William K. Klingaman, *Abraham Lincoln and the Road to Emancipation, 1861–1865* (New York: Viking Penguin, 2001), p. 140.

4. Benjamin Thomas and Harold Hyman, *Stanton: The Life and Times of Lincoln's Secretary of War* (New York: Knopf Books, 1962), p. 239.

5. Abraham Lincoln, "The Emancipation Proclamation," n.d., <http://usinfo .state.gov/usa/infousa/facts/democrac/24.htm> (March 10, 2004).

CHAPTER 5. LET FREEDOM RING

1. John Hope Franklin, *The Emancipation Proclamation* (Garden City, N.Y.: Doubleday & Company, Inc., 1963), p. 95.

2. Geoffrey C. Ward, *The Civil War: An Illustrated History* (New York: Knopf, 1990), p. 177.

3. Franklin, p. 62.

4. Stephen B. Oates, *With Malice Toward None: The Life of Abraham Lincoln* (New York: Harper & Row, 1977), p. 320.

5. Stephen B. Oates, *Abraham Lincoln: The Man Behind the Myths* (New York: Harper & Row, 1984), p. 18.

6. Ward, p. 247.

7. James M. McPherson, *For Cause and Comrades: Why Men Fought in the Civil War* (New York: Oxford University Press, 1997), pp. 122–123.

8. Ibid., p. 127.

9. Lincoln's Second Inaugural Address, March 4, 1865, <http://www.ideasign .com/chiliast/pdocs/inaugural/lincoln2.htm> (October 22, 2003).

10. Oates, *With Malice Toward None*, p. 333.

GLOSSARY

abolitionist—A person who wants to put an end to slavery.

auction—A public sale where property is sold to the highest bidder.

confederacy—People or states that have joined together.

Confederate States of America—The eleven southern states that left the United States to become a separate nation: Alabama, Arkansas, Florida, Georgia, Louisiana, Mississippi, North Carolina, South Carolina, Tennessee, Texas, and Virginia.

emancipation—The act of freeing people.

Emancipation Proclamation—A ruling written by President Abraham Lincoln that freed all the slaves in the rebelling states.

pioneer—A person who explores unsettled territory.

plantation—A large farm, usually in the South.

preliminary—Before; leading up to the main event or announcement.

proclamation—A public announcement.

secede—To break away from.

union—The uniting of a group of people; during the Civil War, the United States was called the Union.

U.S. Constitution—A paper describing the powers of the government and the rights of the American people. It contains the basic laws of the United States.

FURTHER READING

Books

Freedman, Russell. *Abraham Lincoln and Frederick Douglass: The Story Behind an American Friendship.* Boston: Houghton Mifflin Harcourt, 2012.

Krensky, Stephen. *The Emancipation Proclamation.* New York: Marshall Cavendish Benchmark, 2012.

McComb, Marianne. *The Emancipation Proclamation.* Washington, D.C.: National Geographic, 2006.

Putnam, Jeff. *A Nation Divided: Causes of the Civil War.* New York: Crabtree, 2011.

Woog, Adam. *The Emancipation Proclamation: Ending Slavery in America.* New York: Chelsea House Publishers, 2009.

Internet Addresses

National Archives and Records Administration: The Emancipation Proclamation
<http://www.archives.gov/exhibits/featured_documents/emancipation_proclamation/>

Lincoln Papers: Emancipation Proclamation
<http://memory.loc.gov/ammem/alhtml/almintr.html>

INDEX